IMAGES
of America
AFRICAN AMERICANS OF
DES MOINES AND POLK COUNTY

General Notes:
It seems that the pictures were mislabeled (by one off) because most photographs do not match their captions but they do match another caption right next to it. The pager inputted the images next to the most logical caption. Please correct the organization of images if they are placed in error.

IMAGES
of America

AFRICAN AMERICANS OF DES MOINES AND POLK COUNTY

Honesty Parker

ARCADIA
PUBLISHING

Published by Arcadia Publishing
Charleston, South Carolina

Library of Congress Control Number: 2011927450

For all general information, please contact Arcadia Publishing:
Telephone 843-853-2070
Fax 843-853-0044
E-mail sales@arcadiapublishing.com
For customer service and orders:
Toll-Free 1-888-313-2665

Visit us on the Internet at www.arcadiapublishing.com

This book is dedicated to those of the African American community of Des Moines. Without them there would be no reason for this book.

CONTENTS

ACKNOWLEDGMENTS

This book is dedicated to Henry and Minne Wilcots, George Brewer, Hattie Mash, Felix Williams Sr., Mr. and Mrs. Everett Singleton, Rev. B.F. Blanks, and many others whom stories could not be told in this work. To my parents David and Bernice Rhone for without them I would not be a Des Moinian and would not have witnessed the extraordinary history of this city.

For my four sons, Frederick Louis "Rick" Clark Jr., Daniel Lee Tate Mujahid Muhammad, Dennis Lee Tate, and Lloyd Daniel "TJ" Tate III. I hope that they and their generation will not forget where they came from and the people who made their history what it was. My hope is that they pass the knowledge and stories they have learned from their elders to their children so our history is not lost.

I would like to thank the following individuals for use of their personal photos. Bobby Washington, Sherry Singleton, Elaine Singleton, Bobby Parker and LuCinda Mc_____, Margarite Avant, Flip Woods, Eugene Woods, Del Jones, Susan and Robbie Howard, Darryl Roland, Jackie Richardson, and Judy McClain. Without the generous assistance of these individuals this book would not have come about.

I would especially like to thank Bobby Washington for his encouragement and willingness to listen to me complain.

I would like to thank my family for their support and encouragement through this possess.

To elders that inspired this work: My parents David and Bernice Rhone, Mr. Bill and Mrs. Edith Sharp, Mr. Leonard and Mrs. Winfred Sharp, Mr. Bobby and Mrs. Dorothy Parker, and to all the others whose stories help make up the history of Des Moines, Iowa. Images are courtesy of the author unless otherwise noted.

INTRODUCTION

For many people, the symbol often associated with genealogical history is that of a strong, limbed tree with an impressively sturdy trunk and grown from something as small as an acorn seed, drifting until a nurturing place is secured, anchoring stoically in the soil, and thriving through adversity. Branches outstretched in a jumble of fragile, small branches intermixed and intertwined with thick supportive ones. A dense curtain of leaves announces the new and continuous growth. The sun and shadows create deep wells of shade and brilliant bursts of light as though mimicking the darkness of sorrow and the lightness of happiness.

This stoic symbol of historical relevance is much like the history of the African Americans in Des Moines, Iowa and Polk County. Men, women, and children have uprooted themselves from what was familiar, even though it was filled with hardship and sorrow, in order to transplant themselves into what they had hoped would be safe and fruitful new lives. The pioneers who cleared a path for Iowa's current African American population did so with fierce purpose, fortitude, and grit.

Sadly, unknown by many, African Americans in Iowa have a long, rich, colorful, and often gripping history. The growth of the sturdy trunk of our ancestral tree starts with the stories of pioneers Jefferson Logan and Adeline Henderson. Jefferson Logan, born a slave in Missouri, stole his master's horse and daringly escaped to Iowa. It is believed that he joined a band of runaways who arrived in Indianola, Iowa, and eventually settled in Des Moines, Iowa, around 1862. Over the years, he eventually ended up working for the Redman's, a well-known and prosperous family in the 1880s. Adeline Henderson was also born a slave on the McGrudy Plantation in Lynchburg, Virginia, in about 1823. After the Union Army pushed toward the McGrudy Plantation, Mr. McGrudy and several hundred slaves escaped to Missouri. Upon arriving in Missouri, Adeline Henderson escaped to Indianola, Iowa, where her husband left her to join the Colored Troops. Adeline continued on to Des Moines, Iowa, where she died in 1937 at what was believed to be 114 years old.

Later, in Iowa–African American history, as the ancestral history broadens, two of the starting branches on the tree were Robert N. Hyde and J. Frank Blagburn. Robert N. Hyde was born in Virginia near Alexander in 1855 and came to Iowa 1874. An enterprising man, Hyde went into business for himself by starting a small labor office. Then, in 1880, he became wealthy by inventing and patenting his own soap, which by 1890 was being sold in every state in the country. In 1893, he invented and constructed the electric fan and carpet duster machine. He held many leadership roles in political, social, and community organizations and was president of the Afro American Anti-Lynching League in 1894. Also, he was involved in the management of the *Iowa Bystander* newspaper. Frank J. Blagburn was born in Clinton, Iowa, in 1868 and moved to Des Moines in 1875. He attended Wilberforce University in Ohio. Upon returning to Des Moines, he was quickly hired by W.F. Crawford in the Savery House Pharmacy where he studied pharmacology. He was the second colored man admitted to the State of Iowa as a registered pharmacist, and he was the first and only colored pharmacist in Des Moines. In 1893, Frank was unfortunately blinded but continued to be deeply involved in social and community organizations.

To connect the myriad of overlapping branches of our ancestral tree is Lillian Edmunds. Born in 1892, Edmunds was educated as a nurse and pharmacist, but she was not able to secure a job in either vocation due to her race. From 1922 to under death in 1955, Edmunds was the charismatic director of the Negro Community Center in Des Moines, later renamed Willkie House. The dynamic Edmunds was involved in organizing the Iowa-Nebraska Federal of Settlement Houses, she served on the Iowa Commission on Children and Youth, and she was delegate to the White House Conference on Children and Youth in 1950. In 1973, a Des Moines elementary school was named in her honor. She was recognized posthumously by the Iowa Welfare Association for her valued contributions to welfare programs.

It is with great pride that I have come to know and embrace "my" Iowa history. How exhilarating it is to know that through slavery, abject poverty, persecution, and death our heroic ancestors, with unwavering resolve, persevered in finding a place that would provide a fertile space in which to grow and nurture future generations. It is their sacrifices that allow us our achievements and blessed us with the opportunity to prosper. Through them we are provided the opportunity to be great leaders, intellectuals, educators, politicians, musicians, doctors, lawyers, and whatever we choose to be. Our ancestors planted the seed and cultivated a rich history, indeed.

—Jeannette Rhone

One

WHY THEY CAME
PIONEERS

Jefferson Logan and son Clarence are on a hunting trip with the Redman family in 1880. Born a slave in Missouri, Jefferson Logan escaped to Iowa on his master's stolen horse. It was strongly believed that he joined a band of other runaways who arrived in Indianola, Iowa, and continued until they settled in Des Moines, Iowa, around 1862. (Courtesy of the State of Iowa Historical Building.)

Adeline Henderson was born a slave on the McGrudy Plantation in Lynchburg, Virginia, in approximately 1823. After the Union Army pushed toward the McGrudy Plantation, Mr. McGrudy and several hundred slaves escaped to Missouri. Once in Missouri, she escaped to Indianola, Iowa, and her husband left to join the Colored Troops. At the time of her death in 1937, it was believed she was 114 years old. (Courtesy of Des Moines Tribune.)

Robert N. Hyde was born in Virginia near Alexander in 1855. He was taken to Kentucky when he three years old. In 1874, he came to Iowa and made it his home. In March 1877, he went into business and started a small labor office. In 1880, he discovered and patented the great cleaning compound known as H and H and began to manufacture the product, and by 1890, it was sold in every state in the country. In 1893, he invented the electric fan and carpet duster machine. Hyde held many leadership roles in political, social, and community organizations, such as being president of the Afro American Anti-Lynching League in 1894. He also had involvement in the management of the *Iowa Bystander* newspaper. (Courtesy of the *Iowa Bystander*, 1890s.)

Born in 1869 in Decatur county Iowa, John L. Thompson attended Callanan Normal College for one year, and afterwards, he attended Iowa Business College. Thompson taught school in Missouri but returned to Iowa where he attended Drake University, where he spent two years of studying philosophy and two years of law. Thompson graduated in the class of 1898. When he was admitted to practice law, he was at the time the only colored man elected to an official position at the Iowa State Senate, serving as a clerk for two terms. He was also the only colored man to serve as special deputy county treasurer. Thompson served as editor and secretary of the *Iowa Bystander* in the late 1890s. (Courtesy of the *Iowa Bystander*.)

George Woodson was born on January 27, 1866, in Virginia. After graduating from Petersburg College in 1890, he attended Howard University's law school in Washington, DC, in 1896. Woodson came to Iowa with the US Army's 25th Infantry. He eventually served from 1890 to 1893 as a non-commissioned officer in the military and was a Buffalo Soldier. Woodson also was one of the founders of the Iowa Negro Bar and the National Bar Association in 1925. Woodson was a prominent lawyer who practiced across a wide area of Iowa, from the coal-mining towns, such as Muchakinock and Buxton, to Oskaloosa and in Des Moines. (Courtesy Woodson Family.)

Joseph H. Shepard was born in 1854 in Missouri. In 1862, Shepard came to Iowa and to Des Moines in 1864, which made him one of the first African American pioneers in the Des Moines area. Shepard was identified as being instrumental in the growth of the African American community of the city. Shepard worked as a bailiff for the Ninth Judicial District Court for several years. Shepard was very active in community and church functions and was a past grand master mason of the Masonic Lodge of Iowa. (Courtesy of the *Iowa Bystander*, 1890s.)

Image #008 is a duplicate of image #009 on page 12.

Image #009 is a duplicate of image #008 on page 12.

William M. Coalson was born in Missouri in 1854. Coalson came to Iowa in 1862 and to Des Moines in 1875, when the Honorable F.D. Jackson was elected president 1897. Coalson was appointed as his messenger twice before 1886. In 1888, he held similar positions. A past president of the African American newspaper the *Iowa Bystander*, Coalson was well respected in the city. Coalson also served in various positions in local secret societies and social organizations as well as the African Methodist Episcopal (AME) church. (Courtesy of the *Iowa Bystander*, 1890s.)

Image #010 is a duplicate of image #011 on page 13.

In 1868, J. Frank Blagburn was born in Clinton, Iowa, where he resided with his parents until they moved to Des Moines in 1875. Blagburn went to Wilberforce University in Ohio, and upon returning to Des Moines, he immediately was hired by W.F. Crawford at the Savery House Pharmacy and took up the study of pharmacy. Blagburn was the second colored man to be admitted to the State of Iowa as a registered pharmacist, and he was the first and only colored pharmacist in Des Moines. In 1893, Blagburn was struck blind yet continued to be involved heavily in social and community organizations. (Courtesy of *Iowa Bystander*, 1890s.)

In 1862, Anna Lewis-Hall was born in Missouri. Ada Lewis-Williams was later born in 1869. In the 1880s, Anna married local barber Ben Hall, and Ada resided with her grandmother Caroline Lewis and great aunt Adeline Wells. In 1890s, they moved to Des Moines, Iowa. Anna became a proprietor of a popular boarding house in the downtown area. She left in 1913 to move to Moline, Illinois. After Anna's departure, Ada, a entrepreneur in her own right, moved to the Highland Park area and ran her own boarding house. Anna was the mother of Mabel Hall-Coleman, Harry Wells, and Hazeldel Counsins-Warricks. (Courtesy of Bernice Rhone Collection.)

Two

HIS EYE IS ON THE SPARROW
AFRICAN AMERICAN CHURCHES

This is a 1908 photograph of a Sunday school picnic of St. Paul AME church. This church is one of the older African American churches in Des Moines. (Courtesy of the Bobby Parker and Lucinda Parker-McClendon Collection.)

Listed below are the members of the Kyles AME Zion Church 1919 choir. From left to right are (first row) Mrs. Ferguson, Anna Woodford, Jessie Smith, Pearl Taylor, and Ouida Broadus; (second row) Viola Hardge, Agnes Broadus, Clara Smith, and Mrs. Charles Wilson; (third row) Johnnie Broadus, Rev. E.S. Hardge, Charles Wilson, W.J. Clinton, and George Woodfork. (Courtesy of David Clinton.)

Kyles AME Zion Church began in a mission on Fourth and Allen Street in 1915; however, it was not organized until 1916 under Rev. Elias S. Hardge, who named it St. John AME. Zion Church. By 1922, the church's name had been changed to Kyles, and they were located on southeast Eighteenth and Scott Avenues. (Courtesy of Former Kyles Historian Kay Spriggs Collection.)

16

Corinthian Baptist Church was founded in 1898 because there were no Baptist churches in the Des Moines area at that time for African Americans. Here, we see the church sometime in the 1920s. The church was established as the First Baptist Church of Des Moines and was eventually renamed Corinthian Missionary Baptist Church. (Courtesy of State of Iowa Historical Building.)

Pictured here is the Corinthian Church Execelsior Club in the 1950s. Corinthian hosted many groups that not only dealt with the church but also with the community. In this picture, you have, from left to right, Capitola Jones, Sadie Jackson, Hi Potter, Jessie Howard, Dorenza Manuel, Mrs. Norman Olphin, Georgia Jones, Irene Miller, Inez Jones, and Molly Beverly. (Courtesy of the Bobby Washington Collection.)

This choir was organized and directed by Mrs. Anthony at Corinthian Church in the 1960s. (Courtesy of the Judy and Ron McClain Collection.)

Maple Street Baptist Church was organized in 1896 from what was then known as Mount Nebo Baptist Church Mission. The mission was located at East Walnut Street between Fifth and Sixth Streets. In this picture are some of the members of Maple Street. From left to right are Gertrude Barber-Brown, Rev. A Ross Brent, two ladies unidentified, and Edward Brown (Gertrude's husband). (Courtesy of Shelia Brown.)

This picture was taken in the 1950s shortly before Kyles AME. Zion Church moved to its new location. It would be the first and last move away from the South Side of Des Moines to the West Side. (Courtesy of Susie Peavy-Holmes.)

Pictured here is the Burns United Methodist Church, which formed in 1866 in Des Moines with its only address listed as "East of the River." Burns is the oldest African American church in Des Moines, Iowa, and is still active. (Courtesy of the Phyllis Grant-Thomas Collection.)

In this photograph, teacher Judy Rhone is in back row of her Sunday school class at Kyles and is surrounded by her class. Pictured from left to right are (first row) unidentified, Janise Rhone, and Pam Rumley; (second row) Debbie Hayes, unidentified, Gary Patton, Curtis Rife, Stony Gaiter, and unidentified. (Courtesy of the Judy McClain Collection.)

Margaret Rhone also a Sunday school teacher at Kyles. Here, she poses with her class. From left to right are (front row) unidentified, unidentified, Gary Patton, Annette Wade, unidentified, Kim Griggs, and Jeannie Taylor; (back row) Curtis Rife, ? Gaither, Chucky ?, Regina Brown, and Jeannette Rhone. (Courtesy of the Judy McClain Collection.)

Rarely could you get the boys to stand still, but here are some of the boys from Kyles Church in the 1960s. From left to right are Gary Patton, unidentified, Jack Hart, Curtis Patton, John Rhone, and Tony Weeks. The group is standing in front of DuWane Weeks. (Courtesy of the Judy McClain Collection.)

Here is a picture of Kyles AME Zion Church's senior choir in 1966. From left to right are (front row) Opal Western, Bertha Singleton, Jeannette Green, Sandra Robinson, Rev. Oscar Peavy, Kaye Spriggs, Pearl Taylor, Linda White, and Ms. Caroldine; (back row) Mrs. DePatton, James Western, unidentified, Bertha Cassell, unidentified, Judy Rhone, Margaret Rhone, Mary Chambers, and Mrs. Caroldine. (Courtesy of the Judy McClain Collection.)

Kyles AME Zion Church had moved from the South Side of town and is now located in the old Negro Community Center at 907 Fifteenth Street under Rev. B.F. Blanks. The Negro Community Center was torn down, and a new building was constructed. During this time, Rev. Oscar Peavy was the pastor. In this picture, taken in the 1960s, the young ladies are (left to right) Susie Peavy, Elaine Singleton, unidentified, and Linda Hart (holding Ricky White). (Courtesy of the Judy McClain Collection.)

In 1973, Reggie Fowler, Jean Rhone (holding her son Rick Clark), and Todd Fowler pose for Easter Sunday picture. The Fowler boys were sons of long-time church member Tepee Flanigan-Fowler. (Courtesy of the Judy McClain Collection.)

Three

WE ARE ONE PEOPLE
SOCIAL ORGANIZATIONS

The Brotherhood Inc. was organized on March 16, 1932, by 62 individuals. The goal of this organization was "to increase the sum total of happiness of its members and to create an atmosphere of real brotherhood and friendly fellowship through the entire city of Des Moines." (Courtesy of the Phyllis Grant-Thomas Collection.)

The women's department of the Brotherhood Inc. was known as the Sisterhood, and it began on January 27, 1935, as the women's component of the organization. Here, we see the Brotherhood Inc. and the Sisterhood in the 1940's. (Courtesy of the Phyllis Grant-Thomas Collection.)

Organized by the Brotherhood Inc. and Sisterhood, the Mary Star Girls Drill Team was under the direction of Carrie Randle. The drill team performed for many community events. On the far right of the photograph is Phyllis Grant. (Courtesy of the Phyllis Grant-Thomas Collection.)

In this picture from the 1940s, you have the Mary Star Girls Drill Team posing before a performance. (Courtesy of the Phyllis Grant-Thomas Collection.)

Here, we see the Elks Marching Band in 1950s preparing for a parade. (Courtesy of the Robbie and Susie Howard Collection.)

Gilbert Randle was the son of Paul Randle and Minne McDonald Randle, and he was born in Ray County, Missouri, in 1907. Carrie Randle was born to Richard Payne and Anna Scott Payne in Boone County, Iowa, in 1904. Gilbert and Carrie Randle became pillars of the community with leadership roles in many organizations, including the Brotherhood Inc. and the Sisterhood. (Courtesy of the Phyllis Grant-Thomas-Collection.)

Myrodyeen and husband, James Rhone, are enjoying a visit from James's older brother John W. Rhone and his wife, who were from Oklahoma. Myrodyeen was a member of the Order of Eastern Star, and her husband, James, was a member the North Star Lodge No. 2, A&FM, and the Lincoln American Legion Post No. 126. (Courtesy of the Judy McClain Collection.)

John Estes Sr. was born in 1905 in Baxter Springs, Kansas, to Frederick and Mary Opelia Estes. John moved his family to Des Moines and founded Estes and Son Funeral Home in 1939. John Estes Sr. continued to run the funeral until he retired and passed it onto his son John Estes Jr. (Courtesy of the Bobby Washington Collection.)

LaFayette Fowler Sr. and Jr. are standing in front of their funeral home at 1701 East Walker Street. LaFayette "Lafe" Fowler Sr. was born in 1884 to William and Eliza Fowler from Kansas. LaFayette founded the oldest African American Funeral Home in Des Moines. (Courtesy of State of Iowa Historical Building.)

Des Moines different clubs and organizations hosted many events through the history of the African American community. At one such event, taken in the 1970s, you have in this photograph Kaye Spriggs, Linda Carter, and Judy McClain. (Courtesy of the Judy McClain Collection.)

Edith and Bill Sharp were owners of the Sharp's Barber Shop and Beauty Parlor. Sharp's Barber Shop was a fixture on 18th Crocker and just off of Center Street. He was active in many community organizations and held leadership roles in many. Edith Sharp moved to Des Moines from Kansas. She was a liscensed beautican and operated the beauty parlor next to her husband's barbershop. She also was very active in church and community clubs and organizations. (Courtesy of Mrs. Edith Sharp.)

Born Hiawatha "Hi" Bueford on April 17, 1906, in Coffeeville, Kansas, Hi moved to Iowa with her family in late 1919. She was an active member in the Eastern Stars and many other social and church organizations in Des Moines. (Courtesy of the Bobby Washington Collection.)

Isiserettes was organized in 1980 to give the youth in Des Moines something exciting and positive to do. Two of the major goals that were set for the youth were to build character and social skills. The Isiserettes have traveled throughout the State of Iowa as well as the United States, serving as ambassadors for the black community, the City of Des Moines, and the State of Iowa. (Courtesy of Eugene Woods and Felicia Woods.)

The Royal Dukes Social Club was founded by nine former members of an earlier social club, the Dashing Eagles, on a Sunday afternoon in October 1927. The club had disbanded, and some of the members had sought to join the mature and classy Beaux Esprix Club but were turned down. In protest, a few of those men decided to establish their own club for social and civic purposes in the community. The nine men gathered at the home of Don Parker for the purpose of organizing their own club and decided to call themselves the Royal Dukes. (Courtesy of the Judy and Ron McClain Collection.)

Here, you have the wives of the Royal Duke members. (Courtesy of the Judy and Ron McClain Collection.)

Four

STAND UP AND BE COUNTED
COMMUNITY

Pictured here is the YWCA youth group. In the early 1900s, young girls, such as above, participated in many church, social, and community organizations. (Courtesy of State of Iowa Historical Building.)

The War Camp Service Center was established in 1918 for a place for African Americans to meet because they were not allowed to attend events and functions at the white YMCA. Shortly thereafter, the War Camp Service Center became known as the Negro Community Center. (Courtesy of State of Iowa Historical Building.)

This image of Roadside Settlement Home seems to be missing; please provide.

Roadside Settlement House was founded in 1896 by the Kings Daughters Union, a group of church women. The settlement house provided services to the poor in a large brick building at Seventh and Scott Streets. It also offered a public laundry and baths, the city's first branch library, and a gym. During the Depression, Roadside developed its own relief programs, which included paying women 25¢ credits for each hour in sewing class. Credits could be exchanged for food and clothing. Roadside Settlement marked the 50th anniversary of its 1899 incorporation and continued to offer services to the neighborhood until the 1970s. (Courtesy Des Moines Rehabbers Club.)

From left to right are Hazel Catherine Warricks, Donald Warricks, Ada Lewis-Martin, and unidentified. (Courtesy of State of the Bernice Rhone Collection.)

This photograph is from the Eastside Community Preschool. Here, you have a not-so-happy-looking Ron McClain in 1940s. He is in the next to last row second from right. (Courtesy of the Judy and Ron McClain Collection.)

Here, you have Hiawatha Bueford volunteering in a rally for Wendell Willkie in 1940. (Courtesy of the Bobby Washington Collection.)

Lillian Edmunds was born in 1892. Edmunds was educated as a nurse and pharmacist; however, she could not secure a job as either due to her race. From 1922 until her death in 1955, Edmunds was the director of the Negro Community Center in Des Moines, which was later renamed as the Willkie House. Edmunds assisted in organizing the Iowa-Nebraska Federation of Settlement Houses. She served on the Iowa Commission on Children and Youth and was a delegate to the White House Conference on Children and Youth in 1950. A Des Moines elementary school was named in her honor in 1973. She was recognized posthumously by the Iowa Welfare Association for her valued contributions to welfare programs. (Courtesy of Iowa Bystander.)

Pictured here is the Willkie House. It was the Negro Community Center and served the African American community of west Side of Des Moines for many decades. From it's founding as the War Camp Center in 1917 until it became the Willkie House and relocated in 1951. This center served as a meeting place for many community groups. (Courtesy of State of Iowa Historical Building.)

The African American community in Des Moines hosted many events for the betterment of the race. Often, scholarship programs such as this were implemented to assist youth who desired to further their education. (Courtesy of the Bobby Washington Collection.)

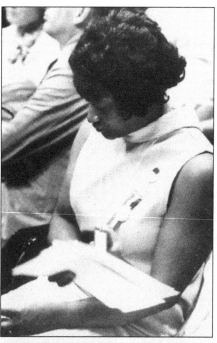

Elleree Avant-Clinton was born in 1922 in Des Moines, Iowa, and graduated from North High School in 1940. Elleree was active in local politics, education, and community organizations. (Courtesy of Margarite Avant.)

Kenneth Perry Whitney Sr. was born October 10, 1921, in Long Island City, New York. After an honorable discharge from the Army, he attended Drake University in Des Moines Iowa, where he received a bachelor's degree. He began working at Willkie House Community Service Center in the 1950s as athletic director, where he inspired and mentored many children and young adults. His teaching career began at Woodrow Wilson Junior High School and Callahan Junior High School. He taught and coached track and field for many years at North High School in Des Moines. Whitney served on numerous committees in the area as well. On December 21, 1999, Whitney passed away. (Courtesy of North High Yearbook.)

Evelyn Davis was born 1921 in the coal-mining town of Hitman, Iowa to Louis Scott and Nettie Fink Scott. Evelyn Davis founded the childcare center Tiny Tots in Des Moines during the late 1960s. Because of her involvement in the community, Evelyn Davis had a clinic named after her in the late 1970s. Currently, there is a park located at Sixteenth and Forest Streets that is named after her. (Courtesy of Edward Davis.)

A lifelong resident of Des Moines, Iowa, Dorothy Turner is the daughter of Dave Turner and Hattie-Doyal. She married local musician Bobby Parker during World War II. (Courtesy of State of the Bobby Parker and Lucinda Parker-McClendon Collection.)

Here are two young girls standing on the steps of the Willkie House. In front stands Janise Rhone, in back Delores Delaney 1960's (Courtesy of State of the Judy McClain Collection.)

In the 1960s, Des Moines saw the destruction of Center Street and the beginning of the work on the Oak Ridge housing project. Pictured here from left to right are Richard Rhone, Nathan Doolin, John Rhone, Tony Hall, and Don Rhone, as they survey the changes in the neighborhood in 1968. (Courtesy of the Judy McClain Collection.)

Born to Jessie and Maureen Frazier, Linda Frazier attended the public schools in Des Moines and graduated from Technical High School in 1962. She married Larry W. Carter, and both became very instrumental in the Des Moines chapter of the National Association for the Advancement of Colored People (NAACP). Linda and Larry held the title of president at one time. They were also very active in church and community organizations. Larry was born in Kansas City, Missouri, in 1937. He moved to Des Moines at an early age and was educated in the Des Moines public school system. He served four terms on the national board of directors for the NAACP. He had the longest tenure of any president in the history of the Des Moines chapter, serving for 12 years in that leadership role. (Courtesy of the Bobby Washington Collection.)

Many African American businesses that had once thrived on Center Street were relocating to University Avenue, where new businesses were opening. Here is Al's Barber Shop, which was0 located on University Avenue with Barbers Hinkey Brewer and Ron McClain. (Courtesy of the Judy and Ron McClain Collection.)

Image #059 does not seem to match the caption.

Sherwood Brown and M.C. Horton stand watch at a Black Pride event in the 1970s. During the 1970s, events were hosted at city parks across the city. Some of those involved in organizing this venture were Harry Flipping, Bill Hunter, Sherwood Brown, and M.C. Horton, to name a few. These events not only kept the summer glowing with positive energy, they also gave those attending memories they would keep forever. (Courtesy of the Robert Simmons Collection.)

Image #060 is a duplicate of image #059 on page 40.

This Black Pride event was held at Goode Park on Seventh Street and University Avenue. (Courtesy of the Robert Simmons Collection.)

Born in Des Moines, Iowa, Robert Simmons is a lifelong resident of the city. In the 1970s, he held a position at the Willkie House and was another unofficial photograph historian of the African American community in Des Moines. (Courtesy of the Robert Simmons Collection.)

Here, you have Tara Wells and Marion Rife posing in front of the Old Dowling gym. (Courtesy of the Robert Simmons Collection.)

Charles "Tuna" Turner poses for the camera in 1975 on Thirteenth and Forest Streets, which was the hang-out place for the young adults at the time. It was here that you went to see and be seen. Charles "Tuna" Turner was once a member of the Mudbone band. (Courtesy of the Robert Simmons Collection.)

Honesty Tate Parker was born as Blossom Jean Rhone and became a community activist, storyteller, and poet. Here, she is a judge at the African American History Pageant in Minneapolis, Minnesota. (Courtesy of Honesty Parker.)

Five

FOR MY COUNTRY I WILL
MILITARY

Lt.Rufus B.Jackson,
Des Moines, Iowa.
370th.Inf.,
Awarded D.S.C.

The only son of Mr. and Mrs. John Jackson of Des Moines, Rufus Jackson graduated from East High School. He entered Iowa State College at Ames. Later, he enlisted in June 1917 in the famous 8th Illinois Colored Regiment. He was appointed sergeant in the Hospital Corp; however, he was promoted to second lieutenant of the same regiment officially known as the 370th Infantry. (Courtesy of the *Iowa Bystander*, 1918.)

Harry Wells was born in Des Moines on Iowa Sept 7, 1890. Other than his time spent in the military, he lived his entire life in Des Moines. He married Bertha Morgan and had six children. Here, you have Harry in 1917 after he had enlisted in the Army. (Courtesy of the Bernice Rhone Collection.)

Pictured here is David Lee Rhone during World War II with group of his army buddies. David is in the last row and on the far right. (Courtesy of the Rhone Family Collection.)

David Lee Rhone was born on March 23, 1918, in Perry, Oklahoma. In 1919, he moved to Des Moines, Iowa, when his father was stationed there during World War I. Here, David Lee is a proud member of the Army. (Courtesy of the Rhone Family Collection.)

Born in Des Moines in 1918, Robert "Bobby" Parker was a musician prior to service and afterwards. He married Dorothy Turner and had two children. He is the son of the musician Vivian Warricks Parker and Theodore Parker, and he was the grandson of William "Professor" Warricks and Mattie Warricks. (Courtesy of the Bobby Parker and Lucinda McClendon Collection.)

Born in Des Moines, Clinton "Big Al" Roland was a local celebrity and was well known in other cities across the country as well. (Courtesy of the Darryl Roland Collection.)

Also a musician from Des Moines, Norvelle White is shown here in the 1940s. He was a sergeant in the military. (Courtesy of the Darryl Roland Collection.)

Pictured here is Sergeant Doyle was the son of Peter and Mary Doyle. (Courtesy of the Darryl Roland Collection.)

During World War II, Fort Des Moines had become the training base for the Women Army Corps. (Courtesy of the State of Iowa Historical Building.)

Born in Des Moines, Harry Jr. followed the footsteps of his father and joined the Army during World War II. (Courtesy of the Bernice Rhone Collection.)

Robert "Bob" Wells attended North High School before joining the Army during World War II. Bob was the second son of Harry and Bertha Wells. (Courtesy of the Harry Wells Family Collection.)

Kenneth Wells, the third son of Harry and Bertha Wells, also served in the military after his graduation from North High School. (Courtesy of the Bernice Rhone Collection.)

Bobby Washington, son of Cary Washington Sr. and Zadia Bueford Bobby, was born in Des Moines in 1934. Bobby Washington joined the United States Air Force in 1950 and served in Korea. (Courtesy of the Bobby Washington Collection.)

Image #077 is a duplicate of image #076 on page 49.

A few years after his brother Bobby enlisted, Ken Washington also joined the military and opted for the Army. (Courtesy of the Bobby Washington Collection.)

Cary Washington, son of Cary
Washington Sr. and Bea Moore,
also joined the Air Force in the
1950s. (Courtesy of the Bobby
Washington Collection.)

Soon after graduation in 1960, Duane
Rhone, son of David and Bernice Rhone,
joined the United States Marines. (Courtesy
of the Rhone Family Collection.)

David Rhone joined the Air Force in 1971. (Courtesy of the Rhone Family Collection.)

Richard Rhone joined the Air Force in the early 1970s and served until his retirement. (Courtesy of Richard Rhone.)

John Rhone joined the Army in the 1970s and served in Germany. (Courtesy of the Rhone Family Collection.)

Blossom Jean Rhone joined the Air Force in 1975. Following basic training at Lackland Air Force Base, she attended school at Lowry Air Force Base in Aurora, Colorado, before going to her permanent base at Homestead Air Force Base in Florida. (Courtesy of the Rhone Family Collection.)

Born in Des Moines, Iowa, to Clinton "Big Al" Roland and Gloria White Darryl, Darryl Roland was active in sport and community activities at a young age. He graduated from Technical High School and served in Vietnam in the 1960s. (Courtesy of the Darryl Roland Collection.)

Six

CONTINUE TO STRIVE
EDUCATION AND SPORTS

Pictured here is football player Leonard Anderson from East High School in 1921. Leonard Anderson was one of the few African Americans on a high school–sport teams at this time. (Courtesy of East High School Yearbook.)

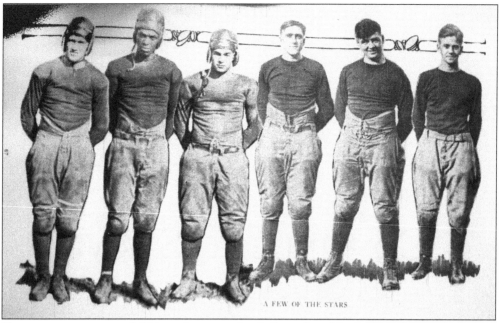

Here, we see an unnamed African American football star from North High School in 1922 (Courtesy of North High School Yearbook.)

First Row: Pearlman, Moffett, Case, Letton, Donohoo, Frowick.
Second Row: Calder, Vandevetter, Rutherford, Loar, Campbell, Mulchay, Webb.

West High School was the forerunner for Des Moines Technical High School. Here, you have Robert Webb (middle row and on the far right) in 1927. (Courtesy of West High School Yearbook.)

Irvin Lee White   Catherine Williams   Loyd H. Wilso

Here, you have Catherine Williams, a graduate from North High School in 1932. Catherine Williams, a leader in social services, has worked for the Iowa Department of Social Services for nearly 30 years and eventually became a deputy commissioner of the department. Born and raised in Des Moines, Catherine became the highest-ranking African American female in state government and one of the highest ranking in social services nationally. She was born in 1914 to Ethel and Godfrey Williams. After graduation from high school in 1932, Catherine pursued her dream of becoming a professional dancer. For 13 years, Catherine danced in New York, Chicago, and Los Angeles. (Courtesy of North High School Yearbook.)

Here, the football team from East High School poses in this 1940 photograph. East High School graduated many outstanding African American athletes. (Courtesy of East High School Yearbook.)

The basketball team at North High School in 1950 included Bobby Washington. Here, he is in the first row and is the second from the left. (Courtesy of the North High School Yearbook.)

Pictured here is the 1951 basketball team at North High School with Sy Forrester. Sy Forrester became the beloved coach at Technical High School in the 1970s. (Courtesy of North High School Yearbook.)

in Assemblies

"North will win!" says Johnny Estes, past North football star as he speaks to the student body in the East vs. North football pep assembly.

John Melvin Estes was born in Missouri to John Estes Sr. and Mildred Young Estes in 1928. Melvin Graduated from North High School in 1946. John attended the University of Iowa. He was a star on the football team until a basketball game at Good Park, where Estes broke his neck and became paraplegic. However, John continued on to Missouri College of Mortuary Science and to Illinois School of Restorative Art. John was a past president of the Des Moines Chapter of NAACP, a founding coach for Des Moines Little League in football, and a lifetime member of the Kappa Alpha Psi Fraternity. He grew up in the funeral home business with his father and worked fulltime serving citizens at Estes and Son Funeral Home until his retirement in 1997. (Courtesy of North High School Yearbook.)

Pictured here in 1957 is the student council of North High School with Madeline Wells. Madeline Wells is the daughter of Harry Wells and Bertha Morgan and was a graduate of North High School. (Courtesy of North High School Yearbook.)

BASIC ELECTRICITY — Row one: Mr. Dowd, Dave Mickle, John Berogan, Mack McLeroy, Dan Shaffer. Row two: George Cobley, Duane Rhone, Robert Corcoran.

Technical High School in Des Moines, which was also nicknamed "Tech," taught students different trades, such as radio and television programming, drafting, tailoring, and electricity (to name a few of the core areas). Here, you have Duane Rhone in the Electricity Core Area at Tech in 1958. (Courtesy of Des Moines Technical High yearbook.)

Here, you have Granville Welch, who was an East High School graduate. Later, Granville Welch taught at Roosevelt High School in the early 1970s. (Courtesy of East High School Yearbook.)

Pictured here is Darryl Roland (No. 67) in the Little League All-American Football SE Bears in 1961. (Courtesy of the Darryl Roland Collection.)

Darryl Roland became a star athletic in high school at Tech. He poses for the camera in this picture from 1965. (Courtesy of the Darryl Roland Collection.)

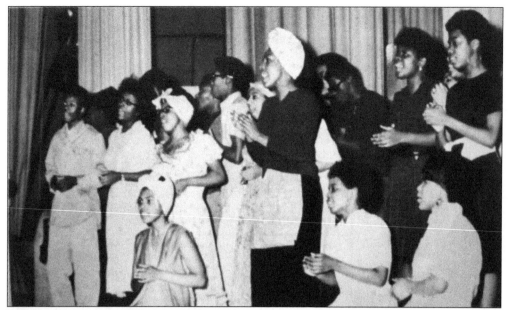

During the turbulent time of the 1960s, pride as a race was demonstrated by the youth through programs such as this Afro American event at Technical High School in 1969. (Courtesy of Des Moines Technical High School Yearbook.)

Some sprinters from Technical High School ham for the camera in this 1969 photograph. From left to right are (front row) Ted Carr, Bob Humburd, Walt Knox, Darryl Duncan, Mike Crawford, and Charles Wolfskill; (back row) Bob Simmons, Howard Kelso, Clifford Terrill, Bill McDonald, Naomis "Beeny" Ward, Bob Hudson, Milton Mosby, and Coach Graves. (Courtesy of Des Moines Technical High School Yearbook.)

This 1969 photograph shows a practice reading at North High School of the play *In White America*, which dealt with issues of the time. One of the students in the play was Clive DePatton, who later, as Kalongy Saddig (a former Black Panther), became a formidable force for the rights of people in Des Moines and a voice for the unheard. (Courtesy of North High School Yearbook.)

Elaine Singleton demonstrates her acting ability and her gift of song as a cast member in the play *In White America*, which staged at North High School in 1969. Elaine is in the last row second from the right. (Courtesy of North High School Yearbook.)

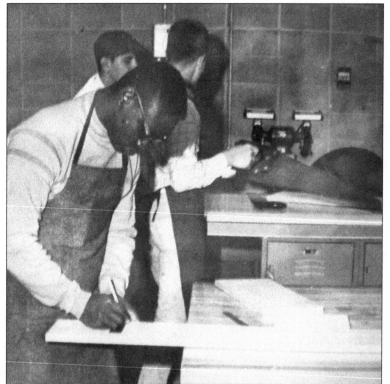

Here, you have Cleo Underwood at Valley High School in 1968. Valley High School is in West Des Moines, a suburb of Des Moines. The African American presence there goes back to the time when West Des Moines was a valley junction. (Courtesy of Valley High School Yearbook.)

Image #105 is a duplicate of image #106 on page 65.

In 1970, Tech student Don Rhone gets ready for radio show. In 1976, Don was the editor of the *Iowa Bystander*, an African American newspaper that was founded in 1894 and still has a presence today. (Courtesy of Des Moines Technical High School Yearbook.)

This play was staged at Technical High School in 1970. In this photograph, from left to right, are (front row) Ted Brown and Barbara Taylor; (back row) Beverly Taylor, Clarence Cavil, and Henry Claytor. (Courtesy of Des Moines Technical High School Yearbook.)

Image #107 is a duplicate of image #111 on page 67.

Cecil Brewton was not only a well-known figure at Technical High School, but he was also a fixture at Goode Park in the 1960s. He is pictured here in 1970. (Courtesy of Des Moines Technical High School Yearbook.)

William Warricks was born in 1892 to William Henry Warricks and Martha "Mattie" Porter. Here, he is a graduate of West High School in 1909. (Courtesy of West High yearbook.)

Pictured here is Betty Hyde at Roosevelt High School in the 1970s. Betty Hyde was the girls' advisor at Callanan Junior High School. She later moved on to Roosevelt High, where she continued to inspire the youth. (Courtesy of Roosevelt High yearbook

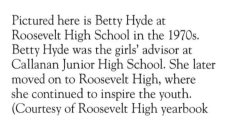

A teacher of drama for 40 years at East High School, Ruth Ann Gaines is well known as a first-class actress. She won a National Teacher Award and is currently serving as a state representative. (Courtesy of the Rhone family Collection.)

In this 1970 photograph, sophomore football players from Technical High School strike poses. Pictured from left to right are Darwin Colton, Raymone Bundy, Rick Singleton, Ed Davis, and Evans Parker. (Courtesy of Des Moines Technical High yearbook

This is a photograph of Denise Williams and Andre Wells in the 1970s. They look refreshed after a track meet. (Courtesy of the Robert Simmons Collection.)

Jeannette Rhone was the youngest child of David and Bernice Rhone Jeannette. She graduated from Technical High School and from the University of Iowa. For well over a decade she had been a fixture at Des Moines Area Community College at the Urban Campus. She is currently the coordinator for the Iowa Life Choices Program. (Courtesy of the Rhone Family Collection.)

Seven

CENTER STREET USA
AFRICAN AMERICAN ENTERTAINMENT OF DES MOINES

This photograph shows a scene from a music festival in Chicago during the 1940s. Pictured from left to right are unidentified, Clinton "Big Al" Roland, unidentified, Thelma "Blucie" Hereford, Cab Calloway, Howard Gray, Catherine Williams, and unidentified. Roland, Williams, and Grey were all from Des Moines. (Courtesy of the Darryl Roland Collection.)

Center Street was the hub of the African American community of Des Moines from at least the 1920s until the 1960s. On Center Street, you had everything you needed. You had doctors, dentists, pharmacists, restaurants, corner stores, a funeral home, and as well as a beauty school. (Courtesy of the Eugene Woods and Felicia Woods Collection.)

Center Street was not just an area of town but a world within a world. When big bands came to town, these nationally known celebrities played at the white hotels and clubs but stayed on Center Street. The likes of Duke Ellington, Louie Armstrong, Ella Fitzgerald, and many more spent many nights on Center Street. (Courtesy of the Eugene Woods and Felicia Woods Collection.)

Ted Brown of the Orlabor Browns is found here at the piano while his wife, Zada, stands close by on far right. (Courtesy of Peter Brown.)

Before the 1960s, you could look north across Center Street from Twelfth Street and see as far as the eye could see. In the 1960s, the freeway disrupted the view just a few blocks north of Center Street. Contrary to popular belief, it was not the freeway that caused the destruction of Center Street. It was local business expansion and the building of a new housing project. (Courtesy of the Judy and Ron McClain Collection.)

Bobby Washington and Aunt Myrodyeen Rhone are standing on the corner of Fourteeth and Center Streets in the 1940s. (Courtesy of the Bobby Washington Collection.)

Pictured here in the 195's are Myrodyeen (left) with brother Omega Bueford and sister-in-law Gertrude "Trudy" Zigler-Bueford. They were enjoying an outing on Center Street at one of the many clubs found there. Myrodyeen's house was on Maryland, which was just around the corner from Center Street. (Courtesy of the Bobby Washington Collection.)

Pictured here are Cary and Bea Washington partying at the Sepia Club in the 1950s. The Sepia was one of the clubs on Center Street. There were many nightclubs and bars on Center Street, but over the years, some clubs disappeared and others changed hands. The Sepia, along with the Billkin, were two of the more popular clubs on Center Street. (Courtesy of the Bobby Washington Collection.)

This picture is believed to be taken at the Sepia on September 8, 1951. From left to right are Lessie Manuel, Albert Garrett, Francis Banks, and Lester Henry. (Courtesy of the Robbie and Susan Howard Collection.)

DORAELVA MACKAY, "Mickey"—Le Cercle Francais 5, 6, 7, 8; French Alliance 3, 4, 5, 6, 7, 8; Forum Club 7, 8; Masquers 5, 6, 7, 8; Amadrams 3, 4; Pas a Pas 3, 4; Girls' Glee Club 3, 4, 5, 6, 7, 8; "Miss Nellie O' New Orleans"; "Jollies" 8; Senior Class Day Committee 8; Intramural Sports 5, 6, 7, 8. Ambition—Social Work and Musician. The life of the social hour.

In this picture from the yearbook of North High School in 1933, you see Doraelva Mackay who graduated in 1933. Dora McKay came from a musical family and sang at church and community events since she was a little girl. In the 1940s, she was the first African American in Des Moines to have her own radio show. (Courtesy of North High School Yearbook.)

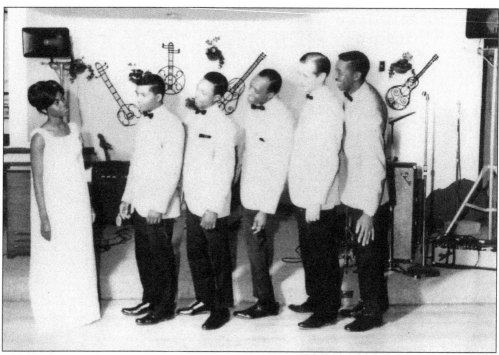

The Soul Brothers and Blues Band was one of the best-known Midwest bands. Here, in this 1966 photograph, are (left to right) singer Anita Cooper, pianist Harlan Thomas, singer Willis Dobbins, backup singer and bass guitarist Ron McClain, lead guitarist Rick Lussie, and percussionist Gene Jackson. (Courtesy of the Judy and Ron McClain Collection.)

Lawrence "Sonny" Davis is the son of Lawrence "Slim" Davis and Wahneta White Davis. He was one of the first blacks to sing on television on the Gordan Gammack Show in Des Moines during the 1950s. He graduated East High School in 1956 and then attended the University of Iowa. He worked as a graphic designer for Disney for 44 years before retirement. Even though he is 73 years old, he is still entertaining. He will release his first soundtrack in Hollywood in 2011. (Courtesy of Lawrence "Sonny" Davis.)

The 1970s was a time of transition for many African Americans of Des Moines. It was a new decade that brought a new style of dress and a different way of acting. The 1960s into the early 1970s were a time of Black Pride and revolution. By the mid-to-late 1970s, much had been mellowed. Robert's Lounge was one of those places to see and be seen. Big Mike sang at different venues in Des Moines. Here, he stands outside of Robert's Lounge on University Avenue in the 1970s. (Courtesy of the Robert Simmons Collection.)

Pictured here is New Establishment in Soul sometime around the 1960s to 1970s. The members of band are Butch Edmonds, James Watkins, Manager Grant Townes, Eddie Thompson, Nick Penny, Ron Langford, Noel Burton, Del Jones, and (not pictured) Marvain Butts. (Courtesy of the Del Jones Collection.)

Pictured here is Split Decision Band during the 1970s, which was a very popular band in Des Moines and surrounding states. The members may have changed over the years, but their sound was always outstanding. Pictured from left to right are Stevie Scott, Gary Jackson, Jaynell Collins, Bob Bennett, Coco Brown, and Del Jones. (Courtesy of the Del Jones Collection.)

The Children of Music was a group of Des Moines musicians who relocated to the Florida area around 1974. The male members of the band are Robert Dawson, Bob A-Genius, Archie Newman, Ronnie McClain Jr., Del Jones, Joe Davis, James Watkins, Pat Singleton, and Ron Langford. (Courtesy of the Del Jones Collection.)

The Children of Music also had two very talented female singers, Elaine Singleton and Marla Kennerly. The singing group eventually relocated to Florida. (Courtesy of the Del Jones Collection.)

This is another picture of Children of Music from the 1970s. Pictured are Pat Singleton, Ron Langford, and Marla Kennerly perform live. (Courtesy of the Del Jones Collection.)

This photograph from the 1970s shows the R&B Band Third World. Pictured from left to right are Eddie Eaves, A. Bach, Tommy Hall, Del Jones, Pat Camp, Kevin Wall, and Chuck Vestration. (Courtesy of the Del Jones Collection.)

In this 1970s picture, you see Verdo White, Unk, Carlo Brown, Kevin Hayter, and Michael McKay hanging out at Robert's Lounge. (Courtesy of the Eugene Woods and Felicia Woods Collection.)

Please consider replacing image #135 with a higher-quality image.

During the 1970s, Robert's Lounge, Black Playboy Club, the Ebony Lounge, and Club John's lined University Avenue from Ninth to Thirteenth Streets. Here, Wanda Oakley is standing in front of Robert's Lounge. (Courtesy of the Eugene Woods and Felicia Woods Collection.)

Like Center Street from the 1930s to the 1960s, Robert's Lounge hosted bands from Minneapolis, Kansas City, Omaha, and as well as from far off Florida and California. This photograph was taken at Robert's Lounge during the 1970s. Pictured from left to right are (first row) unidentified, VonCeel Woods, and Anita Burrell; (second row) Carolyn Fonza, Michael Simmons, and Wanda Oakley. (Courtesy of the Eugene Woods and Felicia Woods Collection.)

This photograph from the 1970s shows the Bueford Clan enjoying a night out on the town. Pictured from left to right are Bobby Washington, Rica Branch, Ted Brewton, Bonnie Sagers, Hi Potter, Benita Woody, Geraldine Webb, and Chauncey Jones. (Courtesy of the Bobby Washington Collection.)

This photograph shows young men out on the town. Pictured are Gerald Williams, Ronnie Shade, and Alonzo Williams, who were going out to the clubs in the late 1960s. During the time in Des Moines, the nightlife was lively and there were numerous things to do and places to go. (Courtesy of the Eugene Woods and Felicia Woods Collection.)

Pictured here are David Williams, Tyrone Helmon, Larry Morrison, and Tommy Fowler outside of Ebony Lounge during the 1970s. Ebony was located across from Robert's Lounge also on Twelfth and University. (Courtesy of the Eugene Woods and Felicia Woods Collection.)

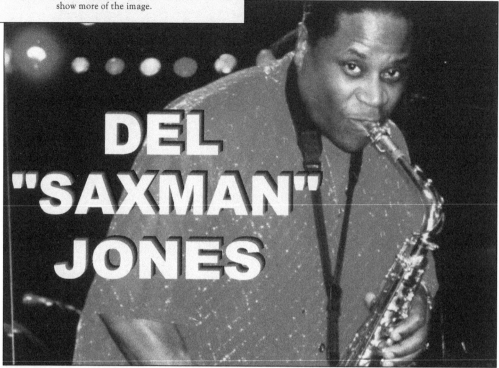

Del Saxman Jones blew smooth jazz, R&B, and pop sounds from his saxophones that were as natural as his heartbeat. After more than 20 years of playing the sax, he is famous for his extraordinary talents as a front man by thrilling audiences with his soulful sax grooves. Del, who is also a record producer, agent, bandleader, and singer, has been performing chart-topping hits on his tenor, alto, and soprano saxophones since age 11. He has played with some of the biggest names in the business, such as James Brown's "Sex Machine," during the last days of the Ike & Tina Turner band, the Presidents' gold hit record "5-10-15-20 (25-30 Years of Love)," Georgio Allentina's "Sex Appeal" that was produced by Prince, and with C.C. Ryder's band. His present creation, FINAL MIX BAND, headlined the grand opening of the Planet Hollywood nightclub in Jakarta, Indonesia, and he toured on the Carnival's new cruise ship *Legend* for several months, traveling to New York, Puerto Rico, Bahamas, Virgin Islands, Bermuda, and Keywest. Jones performed grand openings for world-class Grand Hyatt hotels in Bangkok, Guam, Taiwan, Singapore, and Spain, and he played for the World Economic Forum in Switzerland. (Courtesy of the Del Jones Collection.)

Image #140 is missing; please provide.

Born in 1906 in Des Moines, Pauline Robinson-Brown had a dream of opening her own beauty school. However, she found that she could not gain admission to the cosmetology schools in Des Moines. She moved to Chicago and attended Madame C.J. Walker's Cosmetology School. Upon completion of her training in 1936, Pauline Robinson-Brown returned to Des Moines and opened a beauty shop. She saved her money and was accepted into the cosmetology school in Fort Dodge, Iowa, where she became certified to teach. (Courtesy of the Susie Peavy-Holmes Collection.)

Image #141 is missing; please provide.

Crescent School of Beauty Culture was one of the many African American businesses that lined Center Street. Others were Estes Funeral Home, Bryson's Boarding House, the Elks headquarters, Billkin, and Sepia. For decades, African American businesses lined Center Street. Names might change over the years but there were always restaurants, pharmacies, hotels, or boarding houses that catered to the African American community. (Courtesy of the Susie Peavy-Holmes Collection.)

Image #142 is missing; please provide.

It was not easy for an African American woman in business in Des Moines during the 1930s, but she still pressed on. By 1939, Pauline Robinson-Brown opened Crescent School of Beauty Culture. Eventually, she developed her own line of cosmetics and beauty supplies named Myrise Paule, which proved to be a very successful venture. In 1944, Pauline Robinson-Brown married Major Humphrey who joined her in business (Courtesy of the Susie Peavy-Holmes Collection.)

Here, you have proud students from the Crescent School of Beauty Culture posing for the camera. (Courtesy of the Susie Peavy-Holmes Collection.)

Pictured here in 1963 is Bill Sharp of Sharp's Barber Shop. Though not on Center Street, Sharp's Barber Shop was a block north and was still considered part of the Center Street community. Bill Sharp loved to talk with his customers, and in this photograph, you find him indulging in favorite past time. Sharp's Barber Shop is still located on Eighteenth and Crocker, and Bill Sharp's youngest son Larry currently manages it. (Courtesy of Mrs. Edith Sharp.)

Eight

We are Family
Featured Black Families of Des Moines

Pictured are the Avants and Clintons. Mattie Branshaw married Thomas Avant in Oklahoma and relocated to Des Moines in the early 1920s. Thomas and Mattie were the parents of Donald, Tom, Elleree, Dorothy, Margarite, and Lucille Avant. (Courtesy of the Margarite Avant Collection.)

Image #145 does not seem to match the caption.

Pictured from left to right are (first row) Michael Clinton, John Calhoun, Alice Taylor, and David Clinton; (second row) Erwin Taylor, Bethaline Taylor, three unidentified cousins from Kansas City, and Margarite Taylor. This photograph was taken in the 1960s. (Courtesy of the Margarite Avant Collection.)

Here you have Elleree Clinton and her sister Margarite Avant. Elleree Clinton was involved in many organizations from policies to education. Over the years she received many awards for the positive work she did for the community. Margarite Avant often worked along side her sister, catering to the needs of the community and continuing her position at the YWCA for over 30 years. (Courtesy of the Margarite Avant Collection.)

In the front of this photograph is Vivian Warricks Parker at the Rusk College in the 1930s. Vivian was born in Des Moines to William Warricks and Mattie Porter Warricks. From the time Vivian was a child, she played at many church and community events around Des Moines. She is the mother of musician Bobby Parker. (Courtesy of the Bobby Parker and Lucinda McClendon.)

Pictured here is the Warricks family picture taken around the 1940s. Although most of the Warricks family remained in Des Moines, William Warricks and his family moved first to Canton, South Dakota, then to St. Paul, Minnesota. Pictured from left to right are (first row) Hazeldel Cousins-Warricks holding grandson Richie Adams, William Henry Warricks, Mattie Porter Warricks, and William Porter Warricks holding grandson Richard Adams; (second row) Ann Warricks, Hazel Catherine Warricks, Don Warricks, Vivian Warricks Parker, Bob Parker, Elizabeth "Betty" Warricks, unidentified, Richie Adams, and Carol Warricks Adams. (Courtesy of the Bobby Parker and Lucinda McClendon Collection.)

This is a photograph of Mattie Porter Warricks and William Henry Warricks. William was born in Missouri in 1867 and moved to Iowa where he met and married Mattie in Greenfield, Iowa, on March 19, 1891. Mattie Porter was born in 1871 in Kentucky. Her family moved first to Illinois before settling in Greenfield, Iowa. Upon moving to Des Moines, William and Mattie were involved in many community organizations. Mattie was instrumental in the Paul Lawrence Dunbar Literary Society while William organized many musical groups around Des Moines and came to be called "Professor." (Courtesy of the Bobby Parker and Lucinda McClendon.)

This is a photograph of Bea Moore Washington and her husband, Cary Washington, in later years. Bea Moore was the daughter of Lloyd and Lula Moore and was born in Iowa in 1913. Cary Washington was born in 1911 in Parksville, Missouri, and moved to Iowa in the 1930s. (Courtesy of the Bobby Washington Collection.)

Here you have Ryland and Theresa Washington and their baby. Ryland is the oldest son of Cary Washington Sr. and was born in Parksville, Missouri. Ryland eventually settled in Omaha, Nebraska. (Courtesy of the Bobby Washington Collection.)

Pictured here are Kenny, Cary, and Bobby Washington around the 1950s. Born and raised in Des Moines the three brothers all attended North High school and joined the military from Des Moines. (Courtesy of the Bobby Washington Collection.)

Bobby Washington, George Brewer, and friends get their picture taken with international star Nancy Wilson. Bobby Washington and George Brewer continued to be good friends for decades. Both excelled at sports in high school, and George Brewer was well known for his interactions with the community. (Courtesy of the Bobby Washington Collection.)

The Brown family was from Orlabor, Iowa. Orlabor is a small town where many African Americans settled after 1900 because of the coal mining work found there. Just north of Des Moines, Orlabor is there although much of the town as been swallowed up by urbanization. (Courtesy of Peter Brown.)

Tywayah "Ty" Bryson was born in Stillwater, Oklahoma, to David Lee and Claudia Bueford. Ty moved to Des Moines as a child with her family in 1919 or 1920.

Here is a Bryson family picture. Pictured from left to right are (first row) daughters Vivian Bryson and Garoldine Bryson, and granddaughters Joyce and Ronny Brown; (second row) Tywayah Bryson, niece Benita Woody, mother Claudia Bueford, and daughter Ogretta Bryson. (Courtesy of the Bobby Washington Collection.)

Pictured here are Tywayah Bueford and brother Omega Bueford in the 1930s in Des Moines. The Bueford family moved to Des Moines a decade earlier, deciding to make this new town their home. (Courtesy of the Bobby Washington Collection.)

David Bueford was born in 1866 in Mississippi. Claudia Johnson was born in 1869 and was the daughter of Henry Clay and Zada Bueford, who were also of Mississippi. In 1887, David and Claudia married in Mississippi. The Bueford family lived in Arkansas and Oklahoma before settling in Des Moines in 1920. (Courtesy of the Bobby Washington Collection.)

Zadia Bueford was born in Arkansas in 1902. She married Walter Woody in 1917 in Oklahoma before the Bueford family relocated to Des Moines. Later, Zadia married Cary Washington of Parksville, Missouri. (Courtesy of the Bobby Washington Collection.)

Pictured here are Sequoyah Bueford and his wife, Pauline White Bueford, around 1935. Sequoyah is the son of David Lee and Claudia Bueford. Born in 1916 in Stillwater, Oklahoma, he moved with his family to Des Moines in late 1919 and early 1920. Pauline White born in 1922 in Des Moines; however, she spent some time in Chariton, Iowa. Pauline is the daughter of Mamie Martin and Roy White. Both hailed from Missouri. (Courtesy of Terry Bueford-Mtichell.)

Shari Lu Caldwell was the daughter of Benita Woody. Shari Lu attended North High School before relocating to Ohio with her family. She seldom returned to Des Moines with her children to visit her Bueford family during the summer. (Courtesy of the Bobby Washington Collection.)

What a beautiful wedding day for Sharon and Benjamin Bueford during the 1960s. Both graduates from Des Moines schools, Sharon and Benjamin shine brightly on their big day. (Courtesy of Benjamin Bueford.)

Born in 1871 in Virginia, George Brooks came to Iowa because of the coal mining in 1880s. He died in a mining accident in Buxton, Iowa, in 1917. His wife, Lulu Roland Brooks, and her children eventually settled in Des Moines. (Courtesy of the Darryl Roland Collection.)

Pictured here are William Bryson and his wife, Maggie Roland. William Bryson was born in 1864 in North Carolina. He married Maggie Roland and settled in Iowa. It is believed that William Bryson, like many other African Americans from 1880 to after the turn of the century, came to Iowa to work the coalmines and to provide a better life for his family. (Courtesy of the Darryl Roland Collection.)

Pictured here is Clinton Roland Sr. with two unidentified females. Clinton Roland Sr. is the brother of Lulu Roland Brooks. They also came to Iowa possibly because of the coal-mining opportunity for African Americans in the 1880s to the early 1900s. Here, they settled and raised a family. (Courtesy of the Darryl Roland Collection.)

Lillian White and an unidentified woman are pictured here. Lillian White is the mother of Gloria White Roland and grandmother to Darryl Roland. (Courtesy of the Darryl Roland Collection.)

Gloria White Roland was born in Des Moines. She attended a public school in Des Moines, graduating from East High School in 1943. She married Clinton "Big Al" Roland in the 1940s and continued to live in Des Moines. (Courtesy of the Darryl Roland Collection.)

Here you have the Douglas Edwards Jones family picture (Del Jones's family). Des Moines African American communities were separated by areas. You had the Westside, the Eastside, and the Southside (which were often combined with the Eastside). There were a few that lived in the Highpark area that was north of downtown, the Orlabor area, and the West Des Moines areas. Often, entire extended families stayed on one side of town for generations; however, eventually families moved to other areas. The Jones family was one of the longtime East Side families. (Courtesy of the Del Jones Collection.)

Charles Singleton is the son of Everett Singleton and Bertha Blanks. He was a musician around Des Moines and beyond. Here, you find him in high school honing his talents in the boy's glee club.

Pictured here is Elaine Singleton in 1966. Elaine Singleton is the only girl out of seven children who were born to Everett and Bertha "Blanks" Singleton. Elaine's father, Everett Singleton, was born in 1913 in Hocking, Iowa, to Sam and Minnie Singleton. Elaine's mother was born in 1918 in Kansas but came to Perry, Iowa, as a baby. Her parents were Charles and Birdie Blanks. (Courtesy of North High School Yearbook.)

Pictured here is the sophomore football team from Technical High School in 1970. Pictured left to right are (front row) David Bradley, Allen Butts, Steven Dyser, and Patrick Singleton; (back row) Gary Peters, Don Heard, Ken Johnson, and John Harris. Patrick Singleton is also the son of Everett and Bertha Singleton. (Courtesy of the Des Moines Technical High School Yearbook.)

Glenn Singleton the youngest son of Bertha "Blanks" Singleton and Everett Singleton and a lifelong resident of Des Moines. He was a member of the Kyles AME church and attended Technical High School. (Courtesy of Des Moines Technical High School Yearbook.)

Here is a part of a very large extended family. Pictured from left to right are (front row) Neva Woods and Bambie Woods; (back row) Bambie Lynn Williams, Bear Michael Williams, and John Williams, who is holding Von Ceel Woods. This picture is taken in the 1950s and either on West Fifteenth Street or on the Southside. Though there was a longtime friendly rivalry between the Westside and the Eastside (which included the Southside), no boundary lines could ever keep family apart. In this photograph, you have the Williams (from the Southside) and the Woods (from Westside). (Courtesy of the Eugene Woods and Felicia Woods Collection.)

In this picture, we see (left to right) Rosie Woods, Neva Woods, Felicia Woods, and Donald Avant in the 1950s. The Woods family was a big extended family that included the Woods, Avant, and Williams families and as well as many other families. (Courtesy of the Eugene Woods and Felicia Woods Collection.)

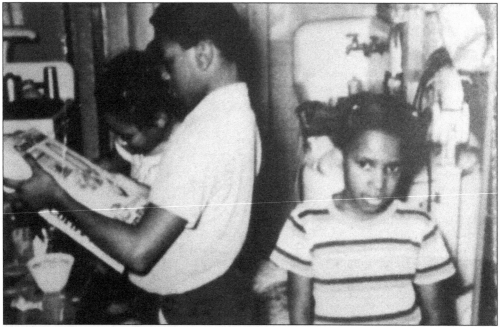

Pictured here are Niva Woods, Donald Avant, and Rosie Woods in the 1960s. Down the street from this family was what was the Negro Community Center, which later became Kyles AME Church. Further up Fifteenth Street, you found yourself on Center Street, which was the heart of the African American community. (Courtesy of the Eugene Woods and Felicia Woods Collection.)

Pictured here is Thelma Woods, who was the sister of Harry, Lance, and Eugene Woods. She lived her whole life in the Des Moines area. (Courtesy of the Eugene Woods and Felicia Woods Collection.)

Here, you have Mabel Williams and Eugene Woods. Mabel Williams was born in 1936 and was the daughter of Felix Williams and Bamie Flanigan. Eugene Woods was her brother-in-law and was an unofficial photograph historian of African American life in Des Moines, Iowa. He is responsible for many photos in the book and passed away during the writing of this book. (Courtesy of the Eugene Woods and Felicia Woods Collection.)

Felicia Woods was born and raised in Des Moines. The daughter of Mabel Williams and Harry Woods, she had taken up the mantle of unofficial photograph historian from her uncle Eugene. She will for some time photograph the African Americans of Des Moines. (Courtesy of the Eugene Woods and Felicia Woods Collection.)

Rosie Burrell was born in 1882 in Fulton, Missouri, to Van and Fannie Burton. Eventually, she relocated to Des Moines where she settled and raised a family. (Courtesy of the Judy and Ron McClain Collection.)

This beautiful woman is an unidentified member from the McClain family. The McClain family includes the Burrells, Vaughns, Burtons, and Maupins, which only names a few of the families that make up this group. (Courtesy of the Judy and Ron McClain Collection.)

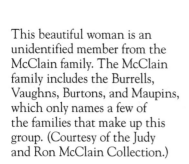

LuWilma Vaughn Hunt was born in 1904.
This photograph was taken around the 1940s
She was the mother of Ardell Maupin, Wanda
"Pookie," Erma, Maxine, and Will. (Courtesy
of the Judy and Ron McClain Collection.)

Ardell Maupin was
born in 1920 to Roy
and LuWilma "Vaughn"
Maupin in Des Moines,
Iowa. She is the mother
of Ron McClain and
the rest of the Williams/
Parker clan. (Courtesy
of the Judy and Ron
McClain Collection.)

Here, you have the Maupin Girls, Wanda "Pookie," Erma, and Maxine. The photograph was taken at 824 Tenth Street in Des Moines and was taken either in the late 1930s or early 1940s. (Courtesy of the Judy and Ron McClain Collection.)

Pictured here are Ron McClain with Wanda "Pookie," Will, and Erma in around 1939. (Courtesy of the Judy and Ron McClain Collection.)

Daughter of Myrodyeen and James Rhone, Blossom was a student at Roosevelt High School. Born in Oklahoma, she relocated to Iowa with her family as a small girl. She is pictured here around the 1930s. (Courtesy of the Bobby Washington Collection.)

In 1955, the Rhone family lived on the Eastside. Pictured from left to right are (first row) Don, Jean, and John; (second row) David Jr. and Richard; (third row) Margaret, Duane, and Judy. The Rhone family migrated from Oklahoma during World War I when James Rhone was station here in 1918. By 1919, Myrodyeen's son David and daughter Blossom followed. Here, they staying with the children, getting married and starting their own families. This is David and Bernice, who are members of the Rhone family. (Courtesy of the Rhone Family Collection.)

Garold Bryson was the owner of numerous businesses, from nightclubs to boarding houses, which were for railroad men. He own property on Center Street but with its demise, he moved his corner store to University Avenue as did other African American businesses. Here, he is in the 1970s with his brother-in-law James Rhone and nephew David Rhone. (Courtesy of the Bobby Washington Collection.)

Bernice Wells Rhone was born August 13, 1920, to Harry and Bertha "Morgan" Wells. She was a lifelong resident of Des Moines. As a nurse's aid at the Iowa Jewish Home, Bernice went on to get her LPN's license and became an evaluator at the Vocational Rehabilitation Center. Upon retirement, Bernice became a foster grandparent and then a senior companion until shortly before her death on March 6, 2010. Bernice is the mother of ten children. (Courtesy of the Rhone Family Collection.)

Pictured in the middle is Catherine Williams with cousin Bernice Wells Rhone and Bernice's daughter Judy Rhone McClain. This picture was taken some time in the 1990s. (Courtesy of the Rhone Family Collection.)

Elizabeth Henry was born in Kentucky in 1894 in Norrisville, Kentucky, to John William and JoAnna "Sweeny" Henry. The family first moved to Kansas then to Iowa where Elizabeth married Robert "Jid Crews" Andrews in 1918. From her union with Jid Crews she had three daughters. Elizabeth died about 1932. (Courtesy of the Jackie Richardson-Bueford Collection.)

Here, you have Lola Richardson and friends in the 1920s. Lola Richardson was born in 1908 in Des Moines and was the daughter of Thomas and Elizabeth Arnold Richardson of Missouri. Lola married Willie Dee "Buddy" Bueford and had a son Lavern Bueford. Eventually, the Richardsons relocated to Omaha, Nebraska. (Courtesy of the Jackie Richardson-Bueford Collection.)

Ida May Crews was born in 1894 in Salisbury, Missouri, to Andrew and Alice Crews. The family moved to Des Moines prior to 1920. In the 1930s, Ida May ran a restaurant on Center Street. She married William Burrell, and the family relocated to Omaha, Nebraska, then to Minneapolis, Minnesota. (Courtesy of the Jackie Richardson-Bueford Collection.)

Joyce Crews born in Des Moines but moved to
Omaha, Nebraska, at a young age. There she
met Lavern Bueford-Richardson (also from Des
Moines) and married him. They eventually made
Minneapolis, Minnesota, their home. (Courtesy
of the Jackie Richardson-Bueford Collection.)

Lavern Bueford-Richardson is
the son of Willie Dee "Buddy"
Bueford and Lola Richardson
and was born in Des Moines,
Iowa. Lavern moved with the
Richardson family to Omaha,
Nebraska. (Courtesy of the Jackie
Richardson-Bueford Collection.)

Here, you have Francis Banks as a child in 1917. Francis Thella Banks was born on April 17, 1911, and passed away September 23, 2003. She was born to Ruth Pittman, and her father was Earl Burns. She spent her childhood in Brookfield, Missouri, but later moved with her mother to Okaboji, Iowa, where she was adopted by George Banks. During her middle-age years, she worked as a buyer and model for a downtown clothing store called Arnolds. Francis married Floyd Lacy and became a mother to her only child, Dolly. Francis spent part of her adulthood in Newton and Colfax, Iowa, where her Banks family lived. She spent her later years at 844 Sixteenth Street in the Sherman Hill area, where she lived for 40 years. "Nan Nan" was how the family knew her best. Cooking, dressing in style, and decorating her home was some of her favorite things to do. (Courtesy of the Robbie and Susan Howard Collection.)

Watsey Humburd was born in 1874 in Mississippi to Thomas Humburd. The family moved to Missouri then by 1900. Watsey and her husband, Jospeh William Winston, were living in Appanoose County. Iowa. By the 1930s, Watsey and family relocated to Des Moines. Here, Watsey is with daughter Lucille Winston. (Courtesy of the Robbie and Susan Howard Collection.)

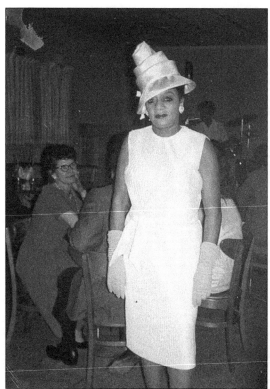

Pictured here is Francis Banks as a buyer for the clothing store Arnolds in the 1960s. She is said to be the first African American buyer for Arnolds. (Courtesy of the Robbie and Susan Howard Collection.)

Here you have Robbie Howard with his siblings and father in this 1960s photograph. Pictured from left to right are Neal, Robbie, and Jane with their father, Jay, in the back. (Courtesy of the Robbie and Susan Howard Collection.)

Sam Setro Singleton was born in 1900 in Monroe County, Iowa, to Samuel and Minnie Henry Singleton. At a young age, Sam became a coal miner and worked in the Hocking Coal Mines in Hocking, Iowa. He eventually moved to Des Moines where he married Betty Blackwell. ((Courtesy of the Sherry Singleton Collection.)

Sitting on the curb on Center Street in 1949 are the children of Sam and Betty Singleton. Pictured from left to right are Sheila, Jim, Pam, and Tim Singleton. Many parades flowed down those streets with blasting music, and young folks in their uniforms marched in step with pride and dignity. That is what this picture reminds me of. Watchin' the parades on Center Streets. (Courtesy of the Sherry Singleton Collection.)

Here are the some of the children of Sam and Betty Blackwell Singleton in 1952. The Singleton children were all born in Des Moines, Iowa, and most continued to make Des Moines their home today. (Courtesy of the Sherry Singleton Collection.)

The entire Sam and Betty Singleton family are pictured here. (Courtesy of the Sherry Singleton Collection.)

Sally Sutton was born a slave around 1834 either in Kentucky or Missouri. She seemed to stay in or around Platte County, Missouri, for most of her life. Late in life, she seemed to have moved to Levenworth, Kansas, where her daughter Lela May Morgan lived. Sallie died about 1910. (Courtesy of the Harry Wells Family Collection.)

Abraham Sutton was the oldest son of Sallie Sutton and was born around 1864 in Leavenworth, Kansas. He was a farmer for the majority of his life. Here, he poses for a rare picture. (Courtesy of the Harry and Bertha Wells Family Collection.)

James Lane, second son of Sally Sutton, was born in 1866 in Leavenworth, Kansas. Sometime in the 1890s, James relocated to Iowa in and around Des Moines. He was a coal miner, and family lore is that he was a cowboy when he was younger, possibly in Texas. For many years he lived in the Orlabor area just north of Des Moines. As James got older, he relocated to the Eastside of Des Moines to be closer to his family. He could be found working his garden and riding his horse. (Courtesy of the Harry and Bertha Wells Family Collection.)

Eliza Sutton born 1868 in Platte County, Missouri. She went to school to be a seamstress in Missouri, where she lived with her mother, Sallie Sutton, until she passed away. Then Eliza lived her sister Lela May Bank and later on with her brother Abe Sutton. Both of her siblings were living at that time in Kansas. After Lela May relocated to Des Moines, Eliza came to stay with her and resided in Des Moines until her death in the 1940s. (Courtesy of the Harry and Bertha Wells Family Collection.)

Pictured here are Anna Sutton Slaughter and her children. Anna Sutton Slaughter was the daughter of Sallie Sutton. From the age of 9 in 1880, she was the servant of Alvin Lightburne, a former slaveholder in Liberty, Missouri. In Liberty, Missouri, Anna Sutton married Isaac "Pluma" Slaughter, as he was called. Pluma and a son died during the influenza epidemic in 1918. Anna continued to work for the Lightburne family for many years before eventually relocating to Des Moines. (Courtesy of the Harry and Bertha Wells Family Collection.)

Here you have Lela Sutton Banks and her daughters Lizzie May and Bertha Morgan. Lela May was the youngest daughter of Sallie Sutton and was born in 1874 in Platte County, Missouri. She relocated to Levenworth, Kansas, where she married. She moved to Des Moines, Iowa, around 1908 or 1909, coming from Levenworth, Kansas, with her two small children, Lizzie May and Bertha. Eventually, she married Ernest Owlsley and settled on the Eastside of Des Moines at 1428 Wayne Street. Lela May Owlsley died in 1953. (Courtesy of the Harry and Bertha Wells Family Collection.)

Image #210 is missing; please provide.

George Wells was born on July 4, 1851, in Kentucky. His mother was Catherine Gamble Young. George, his wife Rachel "Birdie" and daughter Ethel moved to Des Moines in the mid-to-late 1890s from Mexico, Missouri, and here they settled. George held many positions during his life and was a barber in the early 1900s. (Courtesy of the Wells Family Collection.)

Pictured here are Rachel "Birdie" Bates Wells and sister Eveline Bates Caldwell. Birdie was born Rachel Bates in 1861 in Illinois. Her mother was Hannah DeJurnette Bates, who spent her last years in Des Moines with her daughter Birdie. Hannah died in 1910. Birdie married George in Missouri and together, with daughter Ethel, the family moved to Des Moines in the 1890s. (Courtesy of the Wells Family Collection.)

This picture is of cousins Harry Wells, Amos, and Lawrence Caldwell, which was taken in about 1895. Harry Wells was the adopted son of George and Birdie Wells. Here, he is at age five with Eveline Caldwell's sons. (Courtesy of the Wells Family Collection.)

Bertha Eliza Morgan Wells was born as Bertha Morgan on October 1, 1897, in Leavenworth, Kansas, to Willis and Lela May Sutton Morgan. Bertha came to Des Moines as a small child and attended the public schools in Des Moines. In 1916, she married Harry Wells from Des Moines, Iowa. (Courtesy of the Harry and Bertha Wells Family Collection.)

Pictured here are Bertha Morgan Wells and daughter Bernice Wells in 1935. They are standing in front of their house, which was located in the Highland Park area of Des Moines on Amherst Street. (Courtesy of the Harry and Bertha Wells Family Collection.)

www.arcadiapublishing.com

Discover books about the town where you grew up, the cities where your friends and families live, the town where your parents met, or even that retirement spot you've been dreaming about. Our Web site provides history lovers with exclusive deals, advanced notification about new titles, e-mail alerts of author events, and much more.

Find Your Place in History.

CPSIA information can be obtained
at www.ICGtesting.com
Printed in the USA
BVHW011800021221
622778BV00024B/453

9 781531 655112